RUHANI SATSANG SCIENCE OF SPIRITUALITY

By

Kirpal Singh

"Man's only duty is to be ever grateful to God for His innumerable gifts and blessings."

I have written books without any copyright—no rights reserved—because it is a Gift of God, given by God, as much as sunlight; other gifts of God are also free.

—from a talk by Kirpal Singh, with the author of a book after a talk to students of religion at Santa Clara University, San Jose, California on November 16, 1972.

The text of this book is the same as what was published during the lifetime of Master Kirpal Singh. Aside from punctuation and capitalization corrections, no changes have been made to the text. It is exactly the same as what was approved by Master Kirpal Singh.

First American Edition published in 1973

This Edition published in 2007 by:

RUHANI SATSANG®
250 "H" Street, #50
Blaine, WA 98230-4018 USA
www.RuhaniSatsangUSA.org

ISBN 978-0-942735-03-1
SAN: 854-1906

Printed in the United States of America
by Print Graphics Pros • (949) 859-3845

Sant Kirpal Singh passed on from this earth in 1974. As such, He is no longer taking on new people to guide out of this world and back to God. He left many books that explain, as much as can be in a worldly language, the meaning of life. The books and the Ruhani Satsang website http://www.RuhaniSatsangUSA.org/ are maintained to help stir an interest in God and to help people know what to look for in their search for the way back home.

When asked about a successor, we can only offer this quote from the Master:

"Today there is a great awakening beginning. Some have got the answer, some have not, but the search to solve the mystery of life has been born all over the world. The day that question arises in the mind is the greatest day of one's life, for once it is born, it does not succumb until it is satisfied.

So, make your life an example of the teachings you follow — live up to them.

If you have a strong desire to get it, then God Himself will make the arrangements for you."

[Excerpts from a talk published in the January 1971 issue of SAT SANDESH]

Sawan Singh Ji Maharaj
(1858-1948)

*Dedicated
to the Almighty God
working through all Masters who have come
and Baba Sawan Singh Ji Maharaj
at whose lotus feet
the writer imbibed sweet elixir of
Holy Naam — the Word*

Sant Kirpal Singh Ji
(1894-1974)

CONTENTS

The Life and Mission of Sant Kirpal Singh Ji 1

Ruhani Satsang: Science of Spirituality 5

   1. To Ingrain in Seekers after Truth:

      (a) The true understanding of life 9

      (b) The higher values of life 10

      (c) The expansion of the Self 11

   2. The Science of the Soul 12

   3. The Practice of Spiritual Discipline 13

   4. Death in Life and a New Birth 15

   5. The Kingdom of God 17

   6. The Quest for a True Master 18

   7. Surat Shabd Yoga 20

   8. The Essence of Ruhani Satsang 22

Cultural Development Through "Man-Making" 25

Books by Kirpal Singh 31

Sant Kirpal Singh Ji
(1894-1974)

The Life and Mission of Sant Kirpal Singh Ji

Such is the great paradox: The Saint, though exalted, is too humble to parade his riches; and his servants, whose wish it is to reveal him, do not know enough.

SANT KIRPAL SINGH, the great living Master of today, was born in the little village of Sayyad Kasran in the Punjab in India (now in Pakistan) on February 6, 1894. He was blessed with some spiritual awakening from an early age, as well as a brilliant mind and a capacity for sustained hard work. Living the life of a householder and rising to a high position in the Indian Government, he found God in his lifetime and now lives only to share what he has found.

Much of his spare time in his youth was given in selfless service to the poor and the sick, and the rest was devoted to God. It was during these times of silent communion that he prayed to God and no one else to manifest to him direct. His prayer was granted, and from this time on he saw during his meditations the Radiant Form of Baba Sawan Singh, whom he took to be Guru Nanak, the first Guru of the Sikhs. However, it was not until seven years later (in 1924) that he was brought to the feet of Baba Sawan Singh physically, and received Initiation from him. Then began a perfect *Gurumukh-Guru* relationship which continued for twenty-four years; after which the spiritual heritage was passed on to Sant Kirpal Singh by Baba Sawan Singh, just prior to his departure from this world.

Sant Kirpal Singh has been bearing this torch of Spirituality handed to him by his Master since 1948 and has so far initiated approximately 100,000 souls in India and abroad into the Mysteries of the Beyond. He has made three world tours: the first in 1955, the second in 1963-64, and the third in 1972. During these tours, thousands of seekers in Western countries saw with their own eyes a living Master in the flesh for the first time, and their lives were touched and transformed. The Master also served as President of the World Fellowship of Religions from 1957-1971, and since 1970 has been engaged in building a *Manav Kendra* or Man Center in the Himalayas. This center, the first of five projected institutions of its kind throughout India, includes free hospitals, free schooling, housing for the aged, and extensive agricultural activity in addition to the spiritual instruction described in these pages.

By way of concluding this brief life sketch, we would like to quote the Master's own words describing the purpose of Ruhani Satsang, his Mission, and his definition of Spirituality.

PURPOSE OF RUHANI SATSANG: "My Master, Hazur Baba Sawan Singh Ji Maharaj, a perfect Saint, had a great desire to form a common forum or platform, *Ruhani Satsang* [the words mean literally "spiritual gathering"—no denominational or sectarian connotations of any kind], at which all persons, even though professing different faiths and religious beliefs, could be imparted the principles of Spirituality and encouraged to practice spiritual disciplines, in order to gain salvation and peace here and in the Beyond."

HIS MISSION: "To fill the human heart with compassion, mercy and universal love, which should radiate to all countries, nations and peoples of the world. To make a true religion of the heart as the ruling factor in one's life. To enable each one to love God, love all, serve all, and have respect for all, as God is immanent in all forms. My goal is that of oneness. I spread the message of oneness in life and living. This is the way to peace on earth. This is the mission of my life, and I pray that it may be fulfilled."

SPIRITUALITY: "Stripped of all its outer encrustations, spirituality emerges as a science, as scientific as any other, as verifiable in its results. Let any seeker take it up and let him create in the laboratory of the soul the conditions that are prerequisite; as sure as the day follows the night shall he rise into the Kingdom of God."

THE PUBLISHERS

Sant Kirpal Singh Ji
(1894-1974)

Sant Kirpal Singh Ji
(1894-1974)

Ruhani Satsang
Science of Spirituality

RUHANI SATSANG, as the name implies, is a center for imparting purely spiritual teachings and training to mankind, irrespective of class barriers such as caste, color, creed, sect, age, education or avocation. As Nature offers her bounties of light, water and air, etc., freely to one and all, so is Spirituality offered free to all who are anxious for self-knowledge and God-knowledge.

In this age of science, Spirituality too has to be treated as a regular science to make it acceptable to the people. It is in fact another name for the Science of the Soul, but, unlike other sciences, it is very definite and very exact in its premise, theory and practice, and yields verifiable results with mathematical precision. Its history dates back to the unknown past, when man first began to reflect within on the meaning of life. It has ever been the natural urge in man to solve the riddle of life. In every age, sages and seers appeared in different parts of the world and gave out the spiritual experiences which we have with us in the form of the sacred scriptures. We are indeed very fortunate to possess their fine records, for they kindle in us a desire and longing to know, and inspire us with a hope that one day we too can unravel the mystery of life and the purpose of human existence.

So far so good, but beyond this there is no way out. By mere reading of sacred literature, we cannot possibly understand the true import of the esoteric experiences that their authors had within themselves in the silence of their soul. Book learning and worldly wisdom are of no avail in exploring the mysteries of the inner worlds. Reasoning is the help and reasoning is the bar. We may reason things out on the intellectual level, but we cannot go beyond intellect itself. The scriptures cannot talk to us and answer our questions, nor resolve our doubts and drive away skepticism from our minds. They cannot grant us the actual inner experiences recorded in them. What then is the remedy? Are we to float on the sea of life, pass our allotted days in hectic strife, and do no more? Has life no other purpose beyond that of a stage actor, who comes on to the stage, plays his part, and then vanishes to appear no more?

Every problem in life is beset with the difficulties peculiar to it. But it does not mean that these difficulties are insurmountable, or that they should deter us in our search for the Eternal Truth. What one man has done toward this end, another can also do, of course with the proper guidance and help. All that is needed is to make a right approach to the problem in the true spirit of a seeker after Truth. God is great and He has His own ways to fulfill the yearnings of His devotees. There is nothing to despair of. Every Saint has a past and every sinner a future.

We have of course to start with the premise that there is a certain central controlling Power behind all this phenomena, no matter what name we may give to, or what our conception is, of this Unseen Power. We see that the Universe around us is pulsating with life and is a manifestation of the Active Life Principle of this Unseen Power, which appears in so many different forms. However, what this Unseen Power is, and how we may contact it, constitutes the fundamental problem.

A professor of theology, however learned he may be,

cannot with all his power of words and ideas give us this contact. Life comes from Life. One who is embedded in the Life Principle may, if he so likes, grant us a contact with the Life Impulse surging within him. A Master-soul who has realized the Truth in himself can help us to have this realization, and no one else. Self-realization and God-realization are inner experiences of the soul, and cannot be had on the plane of the senses. Inner awareness comes only when we rise above outer awareness. We have first to transcend body consciousness so as to liberate the soul from all outer attachments. The inner man must first be freed from the outer man, consisting of body, mind, sense-organs, the intellect, and the vital airs (physical energies), for none of these can contact the Pure Consciousness; which is wholly non-material in essence, the life of all life and the very soul of all that exists. These are some of the vital problems with which Godmen are concerned.

Ruhani Satsang then deals with the most abstruse prob–ems connected with the soul and primarily imparts instructions in the Science of the Soul. All other con–siderations, physical, social, moral, are secondary and enter discussion only insofar as they aid in the upliftment of the soul. As it is a science of the Beyond, it is called *Para-Vidya*, or the knowledge that the soul experiences directly and immediately, above and beyond the realm of the senses. It seeks to make the human soul one with the Oversoul by transcending the physical plane. The actual awakening of the spirit into its own, its gradual efflorescence into Cosmic Awareness, is the work of the Master Power overhead, and is achieved through a regular process of self-analysis or inversion.

O Nanak! Without an experience of self-analysis, one cannot escape from the delusion of empirical life.

Similarly, Christ said:

> *For whosoever will save his life shall lose it: and whosoever will lose his life for my sake shall find it.*
>
> MATTHEW 16:25

The Path of the Masters needs the guidance and the help of a living Master or Adept, not only to understand the theory, but in order to practice the Science of the Soul. A Master of Realized Truth can not only reveal the true import of the scriptures which otherwise are sealed to us, but can also grant us an inner contact with Truth Itself and make us theists in the true sense of the word. The scriptures to him are just handy aids to enlighten people of different faiths and beliefs. It is on this common ground of Spirituality that men of all faiths can meet together and thus constitute the great family of man. It is Ruhani Satsang that provides this common ground for people of all faiths to gather together for spiritual instruction.

It was ever the desire of my Master, Baba Sawan Singh Ji, to form a common forum where people professing various faiths and religious beliefs or belonging to diverse sects and orders could meet together to discuss the principles of Spirituality and to practice spiritual discipline under the guidance of a Master-soul, thereby gaining salvation and peace, both here and hereafter. A perfect Master is not concerned with the social order of things nor does he interfere in it. He brings from God to His children the message of spiritual emancipation. His is a message of Hope, Redemption and Fulfillment to one and all alike. Such blessed beings are Children of Light and come into the world to diffuse this Light among suffering humanity, as they themselves affirm:

Kabir knows the mysteries of the House of God and brings a message from the Most High.

A Master-soul is known by the catholicity of his teachings, which have a universal appeal for all.

Ruhani Satsang is not concerned with the socio-religious codes of conduct, nor with the performance of rites and rituals, nor with the formal places of worship. The human body is the true Temple of God, and since *God is Spirit, they who worship Him must worship Him in Spirit and in Truth.* Ruhani Satsang is a living embodiment of the teachings and ideals of the Master Saint, Baba Sawan Singh Ji, and is a center where the exposition of his views on life, which pertain to the emancipation of the soul, is given.

The activities of Ruhani Satsang are described under the following headings:

I. To Ingrain in Seekers after Truth:

(a) The true understanding of life—the everlasting and unchanging nature of the soul in the continually changing phenomena of life, which may be compared to the "still point" on the ever-revolving wheel, at once fixed and yet in seeming motion.

> *Except for the point, the still point,*
> *There would be no dance,*
> *And there is only the dance.*
>
> T. S. ELIOT

One learns the true meaning of:

> *That which is born of the flesh is flesh;*
> *and that which is born of the Spirit is spirit.*
>
> JOHN 3:6

> *The life is more than meat,*
> *and the body is more than raiment.*
>
> LUKE 12:23

> *For what shall it profit a man, if he shall gain the whole world, and lose his own soul?*
> *Or what shall a man give in exchange for his soul?*
>
> MARK 8:36-37

(b) The higher values of life—the greatness of God and the need for humility, leading to a pure and honest life of truth, chastity, abstinence, and a loving selfless service of humanity. The practice of moral virtues has always been enjoined by all spiritual teachers, as only an ethical life can pave the way for a spiritual life. Christ promised the kingdom of heaven to the poor in spirit; the kingdom of earth to the meek; mercy to the merciful; and the vision of God to the pure in heart. Before Christ, Moses gave the Ten Commandments to the Israelites; Buddha, the Enlightened One, taught the noble Eightfold Path of Righteousness to those who took to the order of the yellow robe. Zarathustra, Kabir, Nanak, and the Rishis of old said the same things in their own words. So it is necessary for the aspirants to gradually weed out moral lapses, one by one, and to cultivate in their place moral virtues; for which the maintenance of a self-introspection diary is necessary. It is the knowledge of our faults and failings that will make us strive to correct them. This in turn leads to true Spirituality.

(c) The expansion of the Self. In this connection, we have in the Gospels:

> *Love your enemies, bless them that curse you, do good to them that hate you, and pray for them which despitefully use you, and persecute you.*
>
> MATTHEW 5:44

> *Thou shalt love the Lord thy God with all thy heart, and with all thy soul, and with all thy mind. This is the first and great commandment. And the second is like unto it, Thou shalt love thy neighbor as thyself.*
>
> MATTHEW 22:37-39

It is therefore necessary that we must learn to love all living creatures, and more so our fellow human beings, as all are the children of the same Supreme Father. Thereby we are not only true to ourselves, but true to the community, to the nation or country to which we belong; and above all, to humanity at large. This leads to the progressive expansion of the Self until it embraces the entire universe and one becomes a world citizen with a cosmopolitan outlook in its truest sense, deserving of God's grace.

Further, what is the nature of love? It should be an unselfish love, a love which worketh no ill to anyone, a love which fulfills the law of God that enjoins loving service with a pure heart. Such a love is the means to Self- and God-Realization:

> *He that loveth not knoweth not God; for God is love.*
>
> I JOHN 4:8

Hear ye all, I tell you the truth—only those who love can know God.

GURU GOBIND SINGH

Do thou love God; for without love thou canst not have peace here or hereafter.

KABIR

So love God and love all His creation—man, beasts, birds, reptiles—for they are all members of the family of God.

II. The Science of the Soul

As theory precedes practice, it is essential that one must have a crystal clear idea of the theoretical aspect of the eternal truths of life, which are conveyed through the correct interpretation of the various scriptures; the right import of which can only be explained by one who has actually realized Truth for himself and established eternal contact with the Divine Link within him. The ultimate Truth is of course one and the same in all religions; but the sages have described it variously, each according to the measure of his own spiritual advancement on the God-way. One who actually traversed the Path completely is called a perfect Master or *Sant Satguru*. He, being fully conversant with the various details of the journey, can explain matters suitably and reconcile the seeming differences, if any, in the scriptural texts. He is a guide on the spiritual path from plane to plane as the soul, after voluntary withdrawal from body consciousness, proceeds along with Him. The different scriptures are but wares in the hands of the Master for convincing those who have but little faith in one or the other of the religious beliefs. By apt quotations from sacred books of different religions, the Master Saints can emphasize the essential unity of all religions on the common ground of Spirituality; for each embodied soul, after transcending body consciousness, escapes from all denominational labels attached to the physical body. It is a practical question of Self-knowledge, and an actual experience thereof is given by the Master to each individual at the time of Initiation. Testimony is always directly based on first-hand experience and not on hearsay or book-learning.

Sant Kabir says:

> *O Pandit, your mind and my mind can never agree; For you speak of what you have read in the scriptures, while I speak what I have seen.*

In the Holy Granth, the scriptures of the Sikhs, it is written:

> *Listen ye to the true testimony of the Saints, for they give out what they truly see with their own eyes.*

> *Nanak does not utter a single syllable of his own, except as he is moved from within.*

Christ said:

> *I do nothing of myself; but as my Father hath taught me, I speak these things.*

> JOHN 8:28

III. The Practice of Spiritual Discipline

Insofar as the theory of the Science of the Soul is concerned, it is essentially an experimental science and has therefore to be judged on the level of actual experience. It is said that an ounce of practice is better than tons of theory. The scriptures even tell us not to put faith in the words of a

Master Saint unless he is able to give some inner experience of what he talks about. But with all that, one must have at least an experimental faith, so as to do what one is asked to, just for the sake of the experiment itself. The spiritual science, as explained above, is the most perfect and exact in every detail, just as two and two make four. Everyone who has grasped the theory and is receptive can be a direct witness of the inner experience, however little it may be, that the Master gives at the very first sitting.

The Absolute Truth is of course imageless; but the Power of Truth, or God in action, is a vibratory force pervading everywhere. Its primal manifestations come in the form of Light and Sound; and it is for the Master Saint to give an experience thereof by helping each soul to rise above the sensory plane, if only for a short while. If this contact is established on the supersensual plane, one can, under the guidance and with the help of the Master, develop it to any extent he may like. The contacts of Light and Sound are the "saving lifelines" within each individual, and the Master who manifests this Light and Sound is called a Saviour, a Messiah, a Prophet, or anything one wishes to call him. The eternal soul principle is described variously as *Sruti* (that which is heard) in the Vedas; *Udgit* (the Song of the Beyond) in the Upanishads; *Akash Bani* (the Music from the Sky) or *Nad* (Voice) in the later Hindu scriptures; *Kalma* (Divine Utterance) or *Kalam-i-Kadim* (most ancient call) in the Koran; *Sraosha* by Zoroaster; *Logos* or Word in the Bible; and *Naam* or *Shabd* in the Holy Granth, the Sikh scripture.

The ancient Greeks, including Pythagoras, called it "The Music of the Spheres"; the Theosophical writings refer to it as "The Voice of the Silence." And without actual contact with this Divine Power within, the Voice of God and the Light of God, good morals and esoteric teachings by themselves are not sufficient. This is why the Bible emphasizes:

Be ye doers of the Word, and not hearers only ...

JAMES 1:22

IV. Death in Life and a New Birth

The contact with the Divine Link, as described above, comes only when the soul rises from the plane of the senses to above body consciousness, and comes into its own on the supersensual plane, for true knowledge is the action of the soul without the aid of the senses:

Here one sees without eyes and hears without ears, walks without feet and acts without hands, and speaks without tongue;

O Nanak! It is by death-in-life that one understands the Divine Will and stands face to face with Reality.

For this experience, the soul has temporarily to disconnect itself from the body and its different sense organs, the mind and the vital airs, all of which are too gross to contact Truth. In other words, an embodied soul has to disembody itself and become depersonalized before it can come into contact with the Master Power, which is subtle and rarefied. Therefore Guru Nanak says:

Unless one rises to the level of God, one cannot know God.

The Divine Power can neither be comprehended nor apprehended by the lower order of things. With all our righteousness, we are as filthy rags; and when in the flesh, none are righteous. The soul, as it rises above body

15

consciousness, shines forth in its pristine purity, rises into Cosmic Awareness, and feels, as it were, the efflorescence of the microcosm into the macrocosm. It is this which is called *Duaya Janma* or the "Second Birth," i.e., birth of the Spirit as distinguished from the birth of the flesh. The Bible tells us:

> *Except a man be born again, he cannot SEE the Kingdom of God.*
>
> JOHN 3:3
>
> *Except a man be born of water and of the Spirit, he cannot ENTER the Kingdom of God.*
>
> JOHN 3:5
>
> *Flesh and blood cannot INHERIT the Kingdom of God.*
>
> I CORINTHIANS 15:50

Thereafter a person walks not after the flesh but after the Spirit. As the process of soul withdrawal is akin to actual death, one gains victory over death, which is the last enemy of mankind. The daily dying at will takes away the sting of death. We may find references to "death in life" in the scriptures of all religions. Kabir, an Indian Saint of great repute, says:

> *Death, of which the people are so terribly afraid, is a source of peace and joy unto me.*

Dadu, another Saint, affirms:

> *O Dadu! Learn to die while alive, for in the end, all must die.*

In the Koran also, great stress is laid on *Mootu qibal az Mootu*, or death before the final dissolution of the body. The

Sufis lay much store on *Fana* (death to the life of the senses) for gaining *Baqa* (life everlasting). Maulana Rumi says:

So long as a person does not transcend the sensual plane, he remains an utter stranger to the Life Divine.

Similarly in the Gospels, words like "I die daily" and "I am crucified in Christ" occur. Christ's own exhortation to his followers, "If any man will come after me, let him deny himself, and take up his cross daily, and follow me" (Luke 9:23), points to the same thing: viz., a true resurrection from one life to another.

V. The Kingdom of God

The culminating point of the spiritual journey is the Kingdom of God, to which the spirit is gradually led by the Radiant Form of the Master. It is not something external, for all beauty and glory lie within the human soul. Of this Kingdom, it is said

The Kingdom of God cometh not with observation: Neither shall they say, Lo here! or, lo there! for behold, the Kingdom of God is within you.

LUKE 17:20-21

In the Holy Koran, the Kingdom of God is referred to as *Maqam-i-Mahmud* or the praiseworthy station (17:81). It is the Buddha Land of the Buddhists, a sublime state of conscious rest in omniscience, called *Nirvana*.

Through the grace of the Master, the spirit then regains the Lost Paradise, the Garden of Eden, from which it was forced out:

*In flesh at first was the guilt committed;
Therefore in flesh it must be satisfied.*

Having paid the wages of sin through suffering, the process of Karmic reactions is finally liquidated by the power of Naam or Word. Protected and enfolded by the Power of God as manifested through the grace of the Master, the spirit forges ahead unhampered, and finally comes face to face with the Reality. This state of blissful beatitude is spoken of variously as the "New Jerusalem" (where the Christ Power appears once again) ; *Muqam-i-Haq* (the Abode of Truth) ; or *Sach Khand* (the Immortal Plane), a place where there is no sorrow, no taxation and no vexation.

VI. The Quest for a True Master

A living, perfect Master is the be-all and end-all of the spiritual path. He is the greatest gift of God and the greatest blessing to mankind. The importance and necessity of a competent Master cannot therefore be over-emphasized. All the scriptures sing praises of the *Sant Satguru* or Master of Truth, who holds a commission from the Lord to help the souls who yearn for Him and wish to return to the House of their Father:

Without a perfect Master, none can reach God, no matter if one may have merits a million-fold.

It is the fundamental law of God that none can even comprehend Him without the aid of a Master-Soul.

THE HOLY GRANTH

A true Master is Master indeed—a Master in every phase of life. As *Guru* or Teacher on the physical plane, he imparts spiritual teachings as any other teacher would do, and shares our joys and sorrows, helping us at every step in our daily trials and tribulations. As *Gurudev* or the Radiant Form of the Master, He guides the soul on the astral and causal planes. As *Satguru* or the veritable Master of Truth, He leads us into the Great Beyond. Such souls are the salt of the earth and are very rare indeed, but the world is never without one or more of such beings, as God may ordain. The principle of demand and supply is ever at work, in spiritual as in secular affairs. One has however to guard against false prophets or "ravening wolves in sheeps' clothing." How to find such a Master is a difficult problem, but patience, perseverence and judicious discrimination always succeed in the long run. When God's Light shines, It shines forth in fullness and cannot remain under a bushel for any great length of time. "Guru appears when the disciple is ready" is an axiomatic truth. This readiness, Kabir tells us, consists of intense longing, humility, compassion and sincerity. When these virtues adorn an aspirant after Truth, God within him, who is his Controlling Power, directs the Master to find him out wherever he may be.

The scriptures tell us some of the signs whereby one may outwardly discern a true Master:

Never bow ye before him who, while claiming to be a Pir (Guru), lives on the alms of others.

A true Master never displays himself among the people, nor takes delight in popular applause.
He never collects alms nor accepts donations for his own use, however voluntarily made.

He who manifests the Infinite in the finite is Satguru indeed and is a veritable sage.

Take him to be a true Master, who engrafts

thee in Truth and who makes thee peer into the unfathomable and links thee with the Sound within.

THE HOLY GRANTH

All Masters are worthy of adoration, each in his own place and in his own way;

But Him alone would I worship, who is embedded in the Sound Current.

KABIR

A true Master brings the message of Shabd and talks of nothing else but Shabd.

Hail as a Master Divine he who can draw down the Celestial Music from above.

PALTU

VII. Surat Shabd Yoga

No doubt, there are ways and ways of union with the Beloved. But in this age, the most natural form of yoga is the Surat Shabd Yoga or the Yoga of the Sound Current. It can be practiced with equal ease by the young and old alike, and hence it is popularly known as *Sehaj Yoga* or the Easy Path. An initiate in this form of yoga does not, comparatively speaking, have to exert himself much. He is of course to do meditation for two to three hours a day, as enjoined by the Master; which consists of sitting in sweet remembrance of the Lord and in doing mental Simran or repetition of the charged words with the tongue of thought, with the gaze or *Surat* fixed at the seat of the soul located behind and between the two eyebrows. One is not to presuppose, visualize, or clutch to have one thing or another. The opening of the Third Eye is the task of the Master. The moment the Master takes charge of the soul, He guides it both directly and indirectly, visibly and invisibly, on this earth and beyond, in this life and the after-life, and never leaves until the final goal has been attained by the soul. Having had such an experience, one realizes the truth of aphorisms like:

> *Lo, I am with you always, even unto the end of the world.*
> MATTHEW 28:20

> *For he hath said, I will never leave thee, nor forsake thee.*
> HEBREWS 13:5

> *And him that cometh unto me, I will in no wise cast out.*

To meet a Master Saint and get Initiation from him is the acme of good fortune and the greatest blessing. He holds the keys to the Kingdom of God and leads the world-weary and heavy laden back to his Father's mansion. He rediscovers God for man in the secret chambers of the soul. As the Master is the greatest gift of God, so is God the greatest gift of the Master, for it is only by the grace of the Master that one can have union with God. In fact, there is no difference between the two, for:

> *I and my Father are one.*
> JOHN 11:30

> *No man knoweth the son but the Father; neither knoweth any man the Father save the Son, and he to whomsoever the Son will reveal him.*
> MATTHEW 11:27

In the Holy Granth of the Sikhs also it is said:

The Father and the Son are dyed in the same color.

The Father and the Son form a co-partnership.

Hence the need for a really awakened soul, for without him, we continue to grope in darkness and cannot see the Light or have salvation.

Hundreds of moons may shine forth; and thousands of suns may be set aglow; but despite a blinding luster like this, pitch darkness prevails within. Without the Master, one finds not the Way and goes wandering in the dark.
THE HOLY GRANTH

Such a Master-soul may work through a representative in far-off lands and make him a vehicle for the purpose. There is a vast difference, however, between the Master and his representative. The former is perfect in his science, whereas the latter is on the Way, not perfect as yet. So we have always to look to the Master Power working at the chosen pole of the physical Master outside for perfect guidance and help until we can commune with the Master Power within.

VIII. The Essence of Ruhani Satsang

Ruhani Satsang is neither an intellectual nor scholastic system of philosophy, nor is it merely an ethical code of rigid moral virtues, though to a certain extent it partakes of the character of both, insofar as these pave the way for spiritual progress. Spirituality is quite distinct from religion, as it is commonly and popularly known today: a social and moral code of conduct and nothing more. Ruhani Satsang deals with the Science of the Soul or contact with the Inner Self in man. It teaches how the Inner Self can be extricated from the clutches of the outer self, consisting of mind and matter and the outgoing faculties, so as to enable it to be witness to the glory of God, to see His Light and to hear His Voice in the inner silence of the stilled mind. It is an experimental science of practical self-analysis, whereby one gains Self-knowledge and God-knowledge. But this depends solely on the grace of God; for no man, however great his learning, wisdom and knowledge, has ever achieved, nor can achieve, success in this field by his own unaided and unguided efforts. Both God and the God-Way are made manifest by the Light of the Godman, who guides the seeker and helps him to rediscover God within his own self. This is the grand lesson in Spirituality, of which Ruhani Satsang is a living embodiment, seeking to help all aspirants after true knowledge—the Knowledge of Realized Truth—which makes all else to become known and leaves nothing unknown. It is the finale of human existence, an efflorescence into the Divine.

Sant Kirpal Singh Ji
(1894-1974)

Cultural Development Through "Man-Making"

IN THE PRECEDING PAGES, the meaning, purpose, aims and activities of Ruhani Satsang are described and discussed. The emphasis, not unnaturally, was placed on the problems that beset a seeker after Truth and how these problems could be resolved with the help of a living Master who is fully conversant with both the outer and inner difficulties of the practical subject of Spirituality. This is not to say, however, that the Master has no interest in the woes of people who do not wish to take up the Path in earnest. The Master has love for all, and does not limit his benefits to disciples only; although of course they enjoy a somewhat special relationship with him, especially after the change we call death.

Today it is becoming more and more difficult for an honest man to live in the world. Virtue is on the decrease and is to many the object of derision. Vice is on the increase, and its practice is even lauded as a virtue. The moral fabric of society, which is its warp and woof, is becoming threadbare, and if this process is allowed to continue, the fabric will tear apart. Even art, which in former years was a means used to educate people to a nobler way of life, has not escaped this destructive process. In the theater, cinema and television media, the filth and dirt of perverted intellect is spawned forth without let or hindrance. Even the most respected of all educational institutions, the University, is becoming forgetful of its true function, which is to produce the highest type of citizen dedicated to the service of his fellow man.

It is to counteract this pernicious process that Ruhani Satsang has established both in India and abroad, training centers or study circles where man can learn the true values of life as taught from a spiritual standpoint. In these centers, the students are trained and guided by personal classes, through correspondence, and through submission of progress reports. The progress reports detail the success and failures that are experienced in the practical application of the principles of true living, which are taught to the students in such classes.

These classes are conducted by selected initiates of the Master, who have themselves made some progress in the art of "man-making," which is the means of attaining control over the mind, senses and sense-objects, which at present bind the soul in bonds of steel. Without the knowledge of the science of "man-making," mastery over the self or animal man cannot be successfully accomplished; for until this self-mastery is achieved, the higher or spiritual part of man's nature cannot come into play. The most urgent need of society today is the active presence of such people, the more there are the better. As mentioned above, selected initiates of the Master are responsible for the dissemination of the knowledge of "man-making" insofar as they themselves have developed it, under the loving guidance of the Master. It is also the responsibility of some of these initiates to visit the various Satsangs to give talks on the Teachings.

The main mission of Ruhani Satsang is to bring all children of God together on one platform so that they may have the right understanding that they are all brothers and sisters in God. Only on such a platform can true integration be inculcated in the hearts and minds of the people at the level of man, soul, and then God, whom we worship by different names. It is the intention of this aspect of Ruhani

Satsang to help to produce a true Work of Art, that is, a whole man; one freed from the lower passions and instincts which degrade his true nature. Man as intended by God is a noble being with noble qualities and aspirations, directed to the attainment of Self- and God-realization in his lifetime. He is not on this earth merely to eat, sleep, breed, and then die. These are the limits imposed on the lower orders of Creation; but man has the spark of God in him, and he is intended for higher things.

The seekers are trained and disciplined in order that they may elevate themselves physically, morally, and intellectually, which will result in true spiritual progress. This will enable them to face successfully the trials and tribulations that they encounter in their day-to-day living. To help them in this phase of their development, they are enjoined:

(1) To maintain a self-introspection diary, recording their failures in Non-Violence, Truthfulness, Chastity, Loving Humility, and Selfless Service. The gradual weeding out of such failures creates the right environment for the continued growth of the seed of Spirituality, which is implanted in the seeker by the Master at the time of his Initiation.

(2) To be regular in attending Satsang, where the Master gives the right understanding of the Teachings, as well as benefiting those attending by his radiation. In the West, such Satsangs are conducted by Representatives and Group Leaders authorized by the Master for this purpose.

(3) To be regularly devoted to their spiritual practices, both morning and evening. This is done mainly at home, although group meditations are given in Sawan Ashram under the personal direction of the Master.

(4) The singing of and listening to devotional hymns from the writings of the Saints of different religions concerning ethical and spiritual subjects is part of the cultural teaching at Sawan Ashram.

(5) To study the sacred literature and books written by the Master. A monthly magazine, SAT SANDESH, is published in English, Hindi, Urdu, and Punjabi, which helps to channel their thoughts in the right direction by keeping constant, sweet remembrance of the Master.

The end result of the training thus imparted fits an initiate for the inner journey as well as making him a decent, law-abiding citizen, and so an asset to society. Such a one becomes an ideal man, with his physical body in full bloom and his soul full of the glory and intoxication of the Ringing Radiance of God. He sees himself as a part of Creation and wishes, as did Guru Nanak, "Peace be unto all the world over, under Thy Will, O God."

KIRPAL SINGH

*Sant Kirpal Singh Ji
(1894-1974)*

Sant Kirpal Singh Ji
(1894-1974)

BOOKS by Kirpal Singh

CROWN OF LIFE
A comparison of the various yogas and their scope; including Surat Shabd Yoga—the disciplined approach to Spirituality. Religious parallels and various modern movements cited. Paperback; 256 pages; index.
ISBN 978-0-942735-77-2

GODMAN
If there is always at least one authorized spiritual guide on earth at any time, what are the characteristics which will enable the honest seeker to distinguish him from those who are not competent? A complete study of the supreme mystics and their hallmarks. Paperback; 185 pages.
ISBN 978-0-942735-64-2

A GREAT SAINT: BABA JAIMAL SINGH
His Life and Teachings
A unique biography, tracing the development of one of the most outstanding Saints of modern times. Should be read by every seeker after God for the encouragement it offers. Also included, **A BRIEF LIFE SKETCH OF THE GREAT SAINT, BABA SAWAN SINGH,** the successor of Baba Jaimal Singh. He carried on Baba Ji's work, greatly expanding the Satsang and carrying it across the seas. Paperback; 230 pages; glossary; index.
ISBN 978-0-942735-27-7

THE JAP JI: The Message of Guru Nanak
An extensive explanation of the basic principles taught by Guru Nanak (1469-1539 A.D.) with comparative scriptures cited. Stanzas of the Hymns in English, as well as the original text in phonetic wording. Paperback; 189 pages; glossary.
ISBN 978-0-942735-81-9

HIS GRACE LIVES ON
During 17 days in the month of August 1974, preceding His physical departure on August 21st, Kirpal Singh gave 15 darshan talks, mostly in the form of questions and answers, to a small group of His disciples at His ashram in New Delhi, India. These talks have been bound together with the unabridged text from Master Kirpal's address to the Parliament of India and His 1971 afternoon darshan talk, True Meditation. Hard cover and paperback; 17 photos; 203 pages.
Hard cover ISBN 978-0-942735-93-2
Soft cover ISBN 978-0-9764548-3-0

THE LIGHT OF KIRPAL
A collection of 87 talks given from September 1969 to December 1971, containing extensive questions and answers between the Master and western disciples visiting at that time. *A different version of this book was published under the title Heart to Heart Talks.* Paperback; 446 pages; 15 photos. ISBN 978-0-89142-033-0

MORNING TALKS
A transcription of a sequence of talks given by Sant Kirpal Singh between October 1967 and January 1969. "To give further help and encouragement on the Way, my new book *Morning Talks* will soon be available for general distribution. This book, which covers most aspects of Spirituality, is a God-given textbook to which all initiates should constantly refer to see how they are measuring up to the standards required for success in their man-making. I cannot stress sufficiently the importance of reading this book, digesting its contents, and then living up to what it contains." —Master Kirpal Singh
Paperback; 258 pages. ISBN 978-0-942735-16-1

NAAM or WORD
"In the beginning was the WORD… and the WORD was God." Quotations from Hindu, Buddhist, Islamic, and Christian sacred writings confirm the universality of this spiritual manifestation of God in religious tradition and mystical practices. Paperback; 335 pages. ISBN 978-0-942735-94-9

THE NIGHT IS A JUNGLE
A compendium of 14 talks delivered by the author prior to 1972, the first four of which were given in Philadelphia in 1955. The remaining ten talks were delivered in India. All of these talks were checked for their accuracy by Kirpal Singh prior to their compilation in this book. Paperback; 358 pages; with an introduction. ISBN 978-0-89142-017-0

PRAYER: Its Nature and Technique
Discusses all forms and aspects of prayer, from the most elementary to the ultimate state of "praying without ceasing." Also contains collected prayers from all religious traditions. Paperback; 147 pages; including appendix; index of references. ISBN 978-0-942735-50-5

SPIRITUALITY: What It Is
Explores the Science of Spirituality. Man has unravelled the mysteries of the starry welkin, sounded the depths of the seas, delved deep into the bowels of the earth, braved the blinding blizzards of snowy Mount Everest, and is now out exploring space so as to establish interplanetary relations, but sad to say, has not found out the mystery of the human soul within him. Paperback; 103 pages plus introductory. ISBN 978-0-942735-78-9

SPIRITUAL ELIXIR
Collected questions addressed to Kirpal Singh in private correspondence, together with respective answers. Also contains various messages given on special occasions. Paperback; 382 pages; glossary.
ISBN 978-0-942735-02-4

SURAT SHABD YOGA *(Chapter 5 of Crown of Life)*
The Yoga of the Celestial Sound Current. A perfect science, it is free from the drawbacks of other yogic forms. Emphasis is placed on the need for a competent living Master. Paperback, 74 pages.
ISBN 978-0-942735-95-6

THE TEACHINGS OF KIRPAL SINGH
Volume I: The Holy Path; 98 pages.   ISBN 978-0-9764548-0-9
Volume II: Self Introspection/Meditation; 180 pages.
ISBN 978-0-9764548-1-6
Volume III: The New Life; 186 pages   ISBN 978-0-9764548-2-3
Definitive statements from various talks and books by the author, collected to illuminate the aspects of self-discipline pertinent to Spirituality. Relevant questions are answered. Text selections are indexed to a source list at the end of each volume. This collection invites the reader to browse.
Three volumes sold as one book; 464 pages   ISBN 978-0-9764548-4-7

THE WAY OF THE SAINTS
An encyclopedia of Sant Mat from every point of view. This is a collection of the late Master's short writings from 1949 to 1974. Included is a brief biography of Baba Sawan Singh, the author's Master, plus many pictures. Paperback; 418 pages.
ISBN 978-0-89142-026-2

THE WHEEL OF LIFE & THE MYSTERY OF DEATH
Originally two separate books; now bound in one volume. The meaning of one's life on earth is carefully examined in the first text; in the following text, the reader is presented with the whys and wherefores of "the great final change called death." Paperback; 293 pages; plus index for the first text; and introduction.
ISBN 978-0-942735-80-2

THE WHEEL OF LIFE
Available in hard cover; 98 pages plus glossary and index
ISBN 978-0-9764548-5-4

THE MYSTERY OF DEATH
Available in hard cover; 125 pages   ISBN 978-0-9764548-6-1

THE THIRD WORLD TOUR OF KIRPAL SINGH
This book was printed directly from the pages of *Sat Sandesh* magazine, the issues from October 1972 through February 1973, which were primarily devoted to Master Kirpal Singh's Third World Tour. 160 pages, 80 black and white pictures.

BOOKLETS BY KIRPAL SINGH

GOD POWER / CHRIST POWER / MASTER POWER
Discusses the ongoing manifestation of the Christ-Power and the temporal nature of the human bodies through which that Power addresses humanity. "Christ existed long before Jesus." Paperback; 17 pages.
ISBN 978-0-942735-04-8

HOW TO DEVELOP RECEPTIVITY
Three Circular Letters (of June 13, 1969; November 5, 1969; and January 27, 1970) concerning the attitudes which must be developed in order to become more spiritually receptive. Paperback; 20 pages.
ISBN 978-0-942735-05-5

MAN! KNOW THYSELF
A talk especially addressed to seekers after Truth. Gives a brief coverage of the essentials of Spirituality and the need for open-minded cautiousness on the part of the careful seeker. Paperback; 30 pages.
ISBN 978-0-942735-06-2

RUHANI SATSANG: Science of Spirituality
Briefly discusses "The Science of the Soul"; "The Practice of Spiritual Discipline"; "Death in life"; "The Quest for a True Master"; and "Surat Shabd Yoga." Paperback; 29 pages.   ISBN 978-0-942735-03-1

SEVEN PATHS TO PERFECTION
Describes the seven basic requisites enumerated in the prescribed self-introspective diary which aid immeasurably in covering the entire field of ethics, and help to invoke the Divine Mercy. Paperback; 20 pages.
ISBN 978-0-942735-07-9

SIMRAN: The Sweet Remembrance of God
Discusses the process of centering the attention within by repeating the "Original or Basic Names of God" given by a true Master. Paperback; 34 pages.   ISBN 978-0-942735-08-6

THE SPIRITUAL AND KARMIC ASPECTS OF THE VEGETARIAN DIET
An overview of the vegetarian diet containing a letter from Kirpal Singh on the Spiritual aspects, a letter from Sawan Singh on the karmic aspects, and excerpts from various books by Kirpal Singh. Paperback; 36 pages.
ISBN 978-0-942735-47-5

Books, Booklets and Audio-Visual Material of Master Kirpal Singh can be ordered from this address or directly online.

RUHANI SATSANG®
250 "H" St. #50, Blaine, WA 98230-4018 USA
1 (888) 530-1555   Fax (604) 530-9595 (Canada)
E-mail: MediaSales@RuhaniSatsangUSA.org
www.RuhaniSatsangUSA.org

Sant Kirpal Singh Ji
(1894-1974)

Sant Kirpal Singh Ji
(1894-1974)